InterActions
small group series

Opening
Your
Heart
to God

PRAYER

Interactions Small Group Series

Authenticity: Being Honest with God and Others
Character: Reclaiming Six Endangered Qualities
Commitment: Developing Deeper Devotion to Christ
Community: Building Relationships within God's Family
Essential Christianity: Practical Steps for Spiritual Growth
Fruit of the Spirit: Living the Supernatural Life
Getting a Grip: Finding Balance in Your Daily Life
Jesus: Seeing Him More Clearly
Lessons on Love: Building Deeper Relationships
Living in God's Power: Finding God's Strength for Life's Challenges
Love in Action: Experiencing the Joy of Serving
Marriage: Building Real Intimacy
Meeting God: Psalms for the Highs and Lows of Life
New Identity: Discovering Who You Are in Christ
Parenting: How to Raise Spiritually Healthy Kids
Prayer: Opening Your Heart to God
Reaching Out: Sharing God's Love Naturally
The Real Deal: Discover the Rewards of Authentic Relationships
Significance: Understanding God's Purpose for Your Life
Transformation: Letting God Change You from the Inside Out

InterActions
small group series

Opening
Your
Heart
to God

PRAYER

BILL HYBELS

WITH KEVIN AND SHERRY HARNEY

ZONDERVAN®   WILLOW
Willow Creek Resources

ZONDERVAN.com/
AUTHORTRACKER
follow your favorite authors

ZONDERVAN®

Prayer
Copyright © 1997 by Willow Creek Association

Requests for information should be addressed to:

Zondervan, *Grand Rapids, Michigan 49530*

ISBN 978-0-310-26600-6

Interior design by Rick Devon and Michelle Espinoza

Printed in the United States of America

09 10 11 12 13 14 15 • 17 16 15 14 13 12 11

CONTENTS

INTERACTIONS

In 1992, Willow Creek Community Church, in partnership with Zondervan and the Willow Creek Association, released a curriculum for small groups entitled the Walking with God series. In just three years, almost a half million copies of these small group study guides were being used in churches around the world. The phenomenal response to this curriculum affirmed the need for relevant and biblical small group materials.

At the writing of this curriculum, there are nearly 3,000 small groups meeting regularly within the structure of Willow Creek Community Church. We believe this number will increase as we continue to place a central value on small groups. Many other churches throughout the world are growing in their commitment to small group ministries as well, so the need for resources is increasing.

In response to this great need, the Interactions small group series has been developed. Willow Creek Association and Zondervan have joined together to create a whole new approach to small group materials. These discussion guides are meant to challenge group members to a deeper level of sharing, to create lines of accountability, to move followers of Christ into action, and to help group members become fully devoted followers of Christ.

SUGGESTIONS FOR INDIVIDUAL STUDY

1. Begin each session with prayer. Ask God to help you understand the passage and to apply it to your life.
2. A good modern translation, such as the New International Version, the New American Standard Bible, or the New Revised Standard Version, will give you the most help. Questions in this guide are based on the New International Version.
3. Read and reread the passage(s). You must know what the passage says before you can undersand what it means and how it applies to you.
4. Write your answers in the spaces provided in the study guide. This will help you to express clearly your understanding of the passage.
5. Keep a Bible dictionary handy. Use it to look up unfamiliar words, names, or places.

Suggestions for Group Study

1. Come to the session prepared. Careful preparation will greatly enrich your time in group discussion.
2. Be willing to join in the discussion. The leader of the group will not be lecturing, but will encourage people to discuss what they have learned in the passage. Plan to share what God has taught you in your individual study.
3. Stick to the passage being studied. Base your answers on the verses being discussed rather than on outside authorities such as commentaries or your favorite author or speaker.
4. Try to be sensitive to the other members of the group. Listen attentively when they speak, and be affirming whenever you can. This will encourage more hesitant members of the group to participate.
5. Be careful not to dominate the discussion. By all means participate, but allow others to have equal time.
6. If you are the discussion leader, you will find additional suggestions and helpful ideas in the Leader's Notes.

Additional Resources and Teaching Materials

At the end of this study guide you will find a collection of resources and teaching materials to help you in your growth as a follower of Christ. You will also find resources that will help your church develop and build fully devoted followers of Christ.

INTRODUCTION:
OPENING YOUR
HEART TO GOD

If you think about it, prayer is a very *unnatural* activity. In fact, the whole concept of prayer flies in the face of the deep-seeded human value of self-reliance. Prayer is an assault on human autonomy, an indictment on a life whose aim is self-sufficiency. Prayer is an embarrassing interruption to someone who is on the fast track, bound and determined to make it on their own.

Although prayer is alien to our independent human tendencies, each of us has probably reached a point somewhere along the journey of life where we made a decision to cry out to God. We might have looked both ways, blushed a bit, and finally fell to our knees. Hoping no one else would see, we fixed our attention on God and actually prayed.

In that moment, we felt that a serious conversation with God might help our situation. We hoped an honest talk with Him might pay off somehow. And in that private conversation with God, we discovered that we were engaged in one of life's greatest phenomenons.

As we grow in prayer, we discover that God actually wants to be in relationship with us. He is not a reluctant listener, like an exhausted employee at a customer service counter saying, "Now what?" In prayer, God convinces us that He has been waiting for us all along. He will listen to us as long as we want to talk. We matter to Him and He cares deeply about us. In times of prayer, God also assures us that His power is available to us. As we communicate with God we hear Him say, "I can handle this situation, your needs, your hardships; I can handle anything life throws your way."

When we get up off our knees, we almost always feel closer to God. We feel a bit more secure in His love, a little less fearful about our situation. We are much more confident of His involvement in our lives. The phrase in Scripture that sums it up best for me is found in Philippians 4:6–7:

> Do not be anxious about anything, but in everything, by prayer and petition, with thanksgiving, present your requests to God. And the peace of God, which transcends all understanding, will guard your hearts and your minds in Christ Jesus.

Maybe, over the years, you have become a person who prays often and freely. Or you may be someone who has prayed in desperation on a few occasions, but for whom prayer is certainly not a regular occurrence. Perhaps you are just starting to investigate this thing called prayer. Wherever you are in relationship to prayer, this series of interactions will help you deepen your understanding of prayer, your commitment to prayer, and the practice of prayer in your daily life.

I am looking forward with great anticipation to helping each of you discover, throughout these sessions, that true prayer has a way of releasing the life of God in your spirit, of activating and liberating the ministry of the Holy Spirit in your life. I am anxious for you to discover the qualitative difference that will be made in your relationship with God as you learn to talk with God through personal prayer.

Bill Hybels

THE PRIVILEGE OF PRAYER

I want to begin this small group session by asking you to play a word association game. You don't have to say anything out loud at this point, simply think about what your first response is when you hear the word *prayer*. What comes to your mind when you hear this word?

I suspect some people think of guilt. You might feel you don't pray enough. Maybe you used to pray more than you do now, but you've become too busy. You have broken out of all the patterns that used to serve you so well, and you feel guilty for not keeping them up.

Maybe what comes to your mind is being frustrated. You have been praying diligently and it seems like nothing happens. You cry out, but all you get is silence. You lift your voice to God and you feel as if it falls on deaf ears.

Possibly the word that comes to your mind is *apathetic*. You are willing to sit in this group and listen, but you don't have any real strong feelings about prayer. Maybe you tried prayer in the past and it left you cold. Now you don't really care a whole lot about it.

Or maybe the word *prayer* brings to mind being fearful. You don't really know how to pray. You are terrified about the possibility that someone in a group like this might ask you to pray out loud. The very thought causes your throat to get dry and your hands to get sweaty. You feel like your words are clumsy while everyone else prays so naturally.

It has been my experience over the years that whenever I ask a group of people how they feel about prayer, there is always a wide range of responses. Some are very positive and others can be quite negative. However, in most cases the topic of prayer does evoke some kind of response.

A WIDE ANGLE VIEW

1 What kinds of visual images come to your mind when you hear the word *prayer?*

A BIBLICAL PORTRAIT

Read Luke 18:1–8

Read Snapshot "A Contrast, *Not* a Comparison"

A CONTRAST, *NOT* A COMPARISON

 Jesus told the story of the widow and the judge in order to motivate people to pray. Often people read this story as a comparison: The woman represents us and the judge represents God. I don't think this is an accurate interpretation. At the end of the story Jesus says something that tips us off to what the story is really about. He says, "And will not God bring about justice for his chosen ones, who cry out to him day and night? Will he keep putting them off? I tell you, he will see that they get justice, and quickly" (Luke 18:7–8a). This is a tip-off to the fact that this story is *not* a comparison; rather, it is a brilliantly devised, cleverly communicated study in contrast.

Jesus was saying that we are *not* like the widow. As a matter of fact, we are totally unlike, maybe even the opposite of the widow. She was forgotten, abandoned, disconnected, and had no access to the judge. We, on the other hand, are in the family of God if we are in a relationship with Jesus Christ. We are sons and daughters of God. We have been adopted into His family through Christ. We have a favored position before God.

In the same way, God is nothing like the judge. He is not stoic, uncaring, seated behind some intimidating bench. He is not heartless and disconnected. He is not moved to act because He is sick and tired of our nagging. Instead, He loves His people and is deeply concerned about them. We matter to Him, and He wants to answer our prayers.

---

2 If this story is read as a comparison, what do you learn about:

• God (how He feels about us)

- Us (as people approaching God in prayer)

- The reason God answers prayer

3

If this story is read as a contrast, what do you learn about:

- God (how He feels about us)

- Us (as people approaching God in prayer)

- The reason God answers prayer

SHARPENING THE FOCUS

Read Snapshot "A Direct Line"

A DIRECT LINE

I remember something my dad arranged for me and the rest of the kids in our family while we were growing up. My father was a very successful, eccentric, and adventurous businessman who traveled all over the world. There were a lot of people fighting for his time. When you called his office, you had to go through the switchboard and a couple of secretaries before you were able to talk with him. But he arranged to have a private line right on his desk and gave out that number to each of his children. He would often say to us, "Now kids, call me at work, because I would love to hear from you anytime."

My dad died almost twenty years ago, but I can still give you the phone number to that private line. I will take that number to my grave, because I used it hundreds of times. Every time I called I would say, "Are you busy, Dad?" "No, no," he would say, "I'm not busy. Thanks for calling me, Billy. What's on your mind?" Having that direct access communicated value to me.

Over the years I have learned that I have this same kind of access to my heavenly Father. He treats me as a favored son, and He is never too busy to talk with me. As a matter of fact, He is always glad when I dial in!

---

4 How does it make you feel when you realize that you have a direct line of communication to the throne room of God?

If this is true, what keeps us from "dialing in" more often?

Read Snapshot "The Heart of God"

THE HEART OF GOD

In the story recorded in Luke 18, Jesus described the crooked judge as unrighteous, unfair, disrespectful, uncaring, preoccupied, and totally disinterested in the needs of the widow. Why do you think Jesus went to such great pains to describe the judge? Because He wanted us to know that our heavenly Father is *totally unlike* that character. Our God is righteous, holy, responsive, tenderhearted, sympathetic, and kind.

We don't have to wrench a blessing from the white knuckles of a tightfisted God. From cover to cover the Bible teaches that God is giving, encouraging, nurturing, and empowering. He loves to bestow good things on His children.

---

5 God is deeply interested in you. He cares about every detail of your life. How have you experienced the care of God in some of the "little" areas of your life?

6 How has God proved His ability to provide for you in the "big" areas of life?

7 If the story of the widow and the judge is a study in contrasts, how might this impact your prayer life?

8 What is one need you are lifting to God in prayer at this time in your life?

What is one joy for which you are thanking Him?

Using the Direct Line

God has given us a direct line to His throne room. He wants to hear about our joys, victories, and successes as well as about our burdens, concerns, fears, and needs. Through Jesus Christ we can approach Him in prayer at any time. Sadly, we often fail to dial in.

Set aside a specific amount of time to talk with God each day. (It might be only a few minutes.) Then establish a set time to connect with God. It could be early in the morning, over your lunch hour, or in the evening. Commit to dialing in and talking with God every day until your group meets again.

Tell Somebody

Take time in the coming week to tell one person what you have learned about the privilege of prayer. Let them know they have a loving Father who has given them a direct line through Jesus Christ. Who will hold you accountable to follow through on this?

How to Pray Authentically

Reflections from Session 1

1. If you made a commitment to spend time in prayer on a regular basis, how is this commitment going? How have you grown in prayer?
2. If you spent time telling someone else about the privilege of prayer, how did that person respond?

THE BIG PICTURE

There is an old axiom that goes, "If you really want to know something, ask an expert." So if you want to know something about basketball, ask LeBron James. If you want to know something about professional golf, ask Tiger Woods. If you want to know how to lead a successful corporation, ask Bill Gates. If you want to know how politics works, call your senator or congressman.

If you have a cutting pain in your lower abdomen and suspect an appendicitis, you don't call a plumber. If your car is making all sorts of strange noises, you know better than to call your pastor. And if your favorite tree in the front yard is sagging and sick, you would never call a veterinarian. Common sense tells us that when we have a need, we are wise to go to someone who is an expert in that field.

This means, if we really want to learn how to pray, we should go to the expert, Jesus Christ Himself. No one in history has ever understood prayer better than Jesus. No one ever prayed like Jesus prayed. Jesus believed in the power of prayer more than any person who walked the earth.

One day the twelve disciples stumbled upon Jesus while He was in private prayer. They were so moved by His earnestness and intensity that when He finally got up from His knees, one of the disciples timidly asked, "Would You teach us to pray?" It was as if the disciples were saying, "After hearing You pray, we realize we have a lot to learn. We are just beginners—first graders in the school of prayer. Would you teach us to pray?"

They asked the expert, and Jesus answered them. He gave them some specific advice and instruction about authentic prayer. We can learn from their example.

A WIDE ANGLE VIEW

1 Tell about a time you failed to go to an expert and ended up regretting your decision.

Describe a time you sought out an expert and were glad you did.

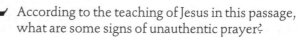

A BIBLICAL PORTRAIT

Read Matthew 6:5–8

2 According to the teaching of Jesus in this passage, what are some signs of unauthentic prayer?

3
What are signs of authentic prayer?

How can you seek to develop these characteristics in your prayer life?

SHARPENING THE FOCUS

Read Snapshot "Pray Secretly"

PRAY SECRETLY

Jesus warned His followers to avoid lifting up prayers on the street corner in a show of spirituality. Instead, He called them to find a private place for prayer. Why the emphasis on privacy? What's this inner room all about? Why is it necessary to go in and shut the door? Certainly one concern was that prayer not to be a show to impress others. Instead, it should be a conversation between us and God.

There is another practical consideration about using an inner room and shutting the door—it ensures a minimum of distractions. I don't know about you, but in my prayer life distractions are deadly. Other voices, music, phones, kids, dogs, birds, almost anything causes me to lose my concentration. Jesus is saying, "Avoid distractions! Find a quiet place, an environment that affords you an opportunity to pray without being interrupted."

I think Jesus is also acknowledging the fact that once we identify a special place for prayer, that place develops a kind of a sacred aura. Your inner room, no matter if it is a laundry room or a study, becomes a special and holy place where you meet with God.

4
What are some distractions you face when you try to spend time in prayer?

What can you do to remove as many of these distractions as possible?

5 If you have a place you get away to pray, describe this place and why it is important to you.

Read Snapshot "Pray Sincerely"

PRAY SINCERELY

Jesus tells His followers they shouldn't use meaningless repetition and empty phrases in their prayers. It is too easy to get caught up in using certain jargon or terminology in prayer. Certain phrases may sound appropriate, spiritual, even pious, but after a while we can find ourselves stringing together a bunch of popular phrases and trying to pass it off as prayer. Heaping up fancy phrases or babbling on and on can't replace heartfelt and sincere communication with God. Jesus invites us to talk with the Father authentically, personally, reverently, earnestly.

6 Why do you think Jesus is so concerned about His followers falling into the pattern of lifting up routine and repetitious prayers?

What are some examples of this kind of prayer?

7 Right on the heels of this teaching about prayer, Jesus gives His followers a model prayer. In light of what Jesus has already said, how did He want us to use the prayer recorded in Matthew 6:9–13?

Read Snapshot "Pray Specifically"

PRAY SPECIFICALLY

For many years it has been a discipline of my life to write out my prayers. I have found the A.C.T.S. formula (adoration, confession, thanksgiving, and supplication) very helpful in the process. These four elements are the primary elements Jesus dealt with in the Lord's Prayer.

The A.C.T.S. process helps me avoid falling into a process of meaningless repetition. My prayer life stays fresh because every day my adoration changes. I have new things to praise Him for each and every morning. When I turn my attention to confession, I try to freely admit my sins to my heavenly Father. With every new day I look back and thank God for what He has done and continues to do in my life. And I also try to list as many specific needs as I can. By putting these on paper, I can go back at a later time and see how my prayers have been answered.

---

8 Adoration is praising God for who He is, focusing on His character and attributes. What quality of God can you praise Him for at this time in your life?

9 Thanksgiving is expressing our heartfelt appreciation for what God has done. What are you thanking God for today?

10 What is one need you are lifting to God right now?

How can your small group members join you in praying for this need?

PUTTING YOURSELF IN THE PICTURE

PUTTING PRAYERS ON PAPER

Write out your prayers for one week, using the A.C.T.S. approach or any other approach that works for you. After you have written your prayer, take time to read it out loud to God.

A PLACE TO PRAY

If you don't have a set place where you try to get away and pray on a regular basis, find one and use it. Commit yourself to being in this holy place for at least five minutes, five times a week. It can be a chair in the living room, a corner of the basement, the cab of your truck, or a swing in the backyard—it just needs to be a quiet place where you will be alone with God. Declare this place to be a sanctuary to God and pray for the presence of God's Holy Spirit to fill that place.

Dangerous Prayers

Reflections from Session 2

1. If you have been writing A.C.T.S. prayers since your last small group meeting, describe how this has affected your prayer life.
2. If you have tried establishing a special place to meet God in prayer, where is this place? How has it become significant to you?

THE BIG PICTURE

There are many different kinds of prayer. Take mealtime prayers, for instance. Everyone knows what those are like. They tend to go really quickly because the food is getting cold. There are bedtime prayers, which usually begin with the phrase "Now I lay me down to sleep, I pray the Lord my soul to keep," and are followed by a series of "God bless Dad, Mom, my pet hamster. . ." and the list goes on. There are also church prayers that focus on the needs of people in the congregation as well as on pressing community and world needs. These prayers can be very meaningful, but often feel very long for parents who are working crowd control on a few high energy kids. Private prayers are prayers you pray when you are by yourself. They often consist of silent cries to God or spontaneous words of praise and thanks. Recited prayers can be very familiar and comforting. And crisis prayers, which can get messy, occur when we honestly pour our deepest hurts and needs out to God. Sometimes, too, we enter into conversational prayer, where we sense God speaking to us in a still, small voice, giving us direction and a clear sense of His presence.

Some kinds of prayer are a little like a 101 or 201 level class. They are rich and meaningful, but they don't challenge us to the deepest level of prayer. In this session we will move beyond dog paddling around the shallow end of the pool and jump into the deep end. In this session I want to invite you to an advanced level of prayer education. The class is called "Dangerous Prayers for Daring Christians."

A WIDE ANGLE VIEW

1 How did you first learn how to pray?

What are some of the earliest memories you have of prayer?

A BIBLICAL PORTRAIT

Read Psalm 139:1–12, 23–24

Read Snapshot "Search Me"

SEARCH ME

A "search me" prayer invites God to aim the searchlight of His brilliant holiness at the inner recesses of our soul and expose whatever is there. When David lifted up his heart in the "search Me" prayer of Psalm 139, he was reflecting on the greatness and grandeur of God. He was declaring the greatness of God and acknowledging that there is no mystery God does not understand. David was praising God for being omniscient, saying, "There is nothing that confuses You about what is going on in the solar system or what is going on in my life. You are intimately acquainted with all my ways." Knowing this truth, David lay his heart completely bare before his Creator and invited Him to search it.

---

2 Why is it dangerous to ask God to search our hearts?

What keeps us from praying this way?

3 What are some of the elements of the prayer in Psalm 139 that seem dangerous to you?

SHARPENING THE FOCUS

Read Snapshot "Break Me"

BREAK ME

Ecclesiastes 3:3 says there is a time to tear down and there is a time to build up. There is a time to pile up bricks and put mortar in between them, and there is a time to get a sledge hammer and to break the bricks apart. After being a Christian for a while, you will discover that you need to develop a whole series of new patterns in your life. To do this, you need God's help. You need to invite Him to break down those things in your life that are not pleasing to Him. You need to learn to pray the dangerous prayer, "Break me!"

4 What is one area in your life that God is breaking down?

What is one area in which you need to ask Him to begin tearing walls down?

Read Snapshot "Stretch Me"

STRETCH ME

As we grow as followers of Christ, we get to a point where we say, "I am no longer content with the status quo in my life. I am tired of being in a spiritual rut." We begin to pray, "God, You created me to be dynamic and growing, but I'm stuck. Please stretch me. Grow me beyond where I am to where You want me to be."

Two thousand years ago a religious leader named Nicodemus stalked through the shadows of the night and asked Jesus to stretch his spiritual understanding. Jesus taught him that no one gets to heaven by just obeying religious laws. He said, "You need to be born again. You need to have an experience with Me, God's Son. You need to repent of sin and receive salvation as a free gift. You need to discover amazing grace." It was a good thing Nicodemus prayed to have his spiritual understanding increased. He might have missed heaven.

---

5 Describe a time in your spiritual life when God really stretched you.

How did it feel at the time you were being stretched?

How does it feel now when you look back on that time?

6 What is one area in your life in which you need to begin praying for God to stretch you?

d Snapshot "Lead Me"

LEAD ME

"God, lead me. I take my life, gifts, talents, resources, energy, and future and put it all in Your hands." That is a dangerous prayer! A couple years after I became a Christian, a deeply committed follower of Christ challenged me to let God lead my life. I was young and somewhat idealistic, so I decided to make a deal with God. I know it is a little dangerous to talk about making deals with God; if it makes you feel better, you can call it a covenant. But, as a young Christian, I called it a deal. I said to God, "I will give you my whole life. You can lead my life until it seems to me you are untrustworthy, and then all bets are off." This "lead me" prayer took all the faith I could muster. Let me tell you, God has been totally trustworthy. He has led me every step of the way.

7 How have you experienced God's clear leading in your life?

8 Put your finger on one area of your life you need to turn over to God and allow Him to start leading you.

PUTTING YOURSELF IN THE PICTURE

SEARCH ME

Take time in the coming week to quiet your heart before God and pray for Him to search you. You might want to begin by reading Psalm 139 again. After you ask God to shine His light on your heart and search you, listen for His voice to speak. Where do you feel conviction of sin? In which areas does He want you to grow? What do you need to confess? What needs to change in your life? Take a blank sheet of paper and write down these things as they come to you. If you ask God to search your heart and He reveals an area He wants you to grow in, commit yourself to respond to His leading.

LEAD ME

Identify one specific area in which you need God to lead you. Pray for God's leading every day until you have clear direction. Ask at least one or two other believers to join you in praying for God's guidance in this area of your life.

THE MYSTERY OF UNANSWERED PRAYER

REFLECTIONS FROM SESSION 3

1. If you have been entering the realm of "search me" prayers, how has God spoken to you? What is one area of your life in which He has called you to grow?
2. If you have been praying "lead me" or "stretch me" prayers, what new (or old) directions has God given you for your life?

THE BIG PICTURE

It's an almost weekly occurrence. The conversation goes something like this: "Bill, didn't Jesus say, 'Ask and it will be given. Seek and you will find. Knock and the door will be opened?'" Being fairly confident of where the conversation is going, I sometimes jump ahead of the person with whom I am talking and say, "Friend, what prayer have you been praying that you fear God is not answering?" It is amazing how often my direct response opens the door for an honest outpouring of confusion and frustration. In these moments I am reminded how many people struggle with the mystery of unanswered prayer.

In most cases the person can identify specific prayers he or she is lifting to heaven, but feels God is not answering. These "unanswered" prayers take countless shapes and forms. "I have been praying for my husband to stop drinking, and he hasn't stopped." "I've been praying for a job, but no matter what I try, I can't find one." "I've been praying for guidance, but I have no idea what God wants me to do." "I have been praying for a friend to become a follower of Christ, but he remains hard-hearted and resistant." The laments go on and on. Week after week, month after month, year after year I hear the same complaint: "God does not seem to be answering my prayers."

The agony of unanswered prayer is deep and chronic for many people. In some cases, the heartache related to this topic can cause people ultimately to stop praying. The mystery of unanswered prayer is one that can baffle, confuse, and frustrate all of us.

A WIDE ANGLE VIEW

1

What is one prayer you lifted to God that seemed unanswered, and later you were glad it wasn't answered?

A BIBLICAL PORTRAIT

Read Mark 10:35–45

2

Imagine you were James or John in this situation. How would you have felt after Jesus responded to your request?

If you were James or John, what might you have learned from this experience?

3 Why did Jesus refuse the request of James and John?

SHARPENING THE FOCUS

Read Snapshot "If the Request Is Wrong, God Says, 'No!'"

IF THE REQUEST IS WRONG, GOD SAYS, "NO!"

When our request is wrong, God will say no! When Jesus and the disciples were denied a travel permit through a certain part of Samaria, the denial aggravated the disciples so much that they requested Jesus to destroy the entire region with fire from heaven. Jesus' reply: "I didn't come to torch people, I came to transform them. No, I'm not going to grant that request."

Do you see the point? Sometimes what seems to be an unanswered prayer is actually a clearly answered prayer. It's just that the answer is no. We are all capable of making requests that are totally self-serving or patently materialistic. We can ask things of God that are shortsighted and immature. We can even pray for things that may appear to be right and good things (like healing). But our God loves us too much to say yes to every request. In hindsight, we should thank Him for saying no—it is a reminder of His wisdom and love.

4 What is one prayer you asked that you know God answered by saying no?

Looking back, why do you think God said no to this request?

5 We can almost expect God to answer certain kinds of prayers with a no. What are some of these types of prayers?

Read Snapshot "If the Timing Is Wrong, God Says, 'Slow!'"

IF THE TIMING IS WRONG, GOD SAYS, "SLOW!"

Imagine leaving on a five-hundred-mile trip in the car with two young children. You are fifteen miles into the trip and the kids are already saying, "Are we there yet? Come on, hurry it up. Drive faster! Is this going to be a long trip?" Let's face it, kids are not good at being patient.

Well, guess what? There is a little child in all of us that wants God to meet every need, grant every request, move every mountain, and do it now! When our all-knowing, all-wise, loving heavenly Father tells us we need to be patient, we can turn seven years old. "But, God, I want it right now! Don't you understand how badly I need it? I can't wait a week, a month, or a year. I need it now!"

God is no more intimidated by these childish fixations on instant gratification than our earthly parents were. He chooses, from time to time, to tell us we need to wait. He does not explain Himself or seek to justify His decision. Remember, He is God! He simply tells us, "Slow down and wait on My timing."

6

Tell about a prayer need you lifted to God for which you had to wait a long time for His answer.

What did you learn over your months or years of slowing down and waiting on God's answer?

Read Snapshot "If You Are Wrong, God Will Say, 'Grow!'"

IF YOU ARE WRONG, GOD WILL SAY, "GROW!"

At times when we are not ready to receive God's answer to prayer, He tells us we need to grow. It is a lot easier to point the finger at God for not answering prayer than it is to look in the mirror and to say that maybe we're part of the problem. Rather than taking an honest spiritual inventory of our lives, we quickly blame God for not delivering the goods.

Psalm 66:18 says, "If I had cherished sin in my heart, the LORD would not have listened." Matthew 5:23–24 warns that if there is relational discord in our lives, we can be cut off from close fellowship with God. It continues by saying we should drop everything and attempt to reconcile those relationships. Then we should go back to the altar, bringing our worship and prayers. And if those passages aren't sobering enough, 1 Peter 3:7 says, "Husbands, in the same way be considerate as you live with your wives, and treat them with respect as the weaker partner and as heirs with you of the gracious gift of life, *so that nothing will hinder your prayers.*" These passages give us a healthy reminder of the need to examine our hearts and lives as we grow in prayer.

7 Why is honest self-appraisal essential as you grow in your prayer life?

8 Take time for silent prayer and for listening to the Spirit of God. Ask the Lord to search your heart and life, revealing anything that might be standing between you and Him. Humbly invite God to shed light on any area of darkness that could be acting as a barrier in your prayer life.

If you feel led by God, communicate to your group an obstacle or area of sin in your life that is hindering your prayer life. Invite the group to pray for you and support you as you surrender this area to God's involvement.

PUTTING YOURSELF IN THE PICTURE

A STRANGE KIND OF THANK YOU

Take time in the coming week to reflect on some of the prayers you have asked over the years that God answered by saying no. Thank Him for His wisdom and for loving you enough to protect you from your own prayers.

WILLING AND WAITING

Identify one or two prayers that you have been lifting to God for a long period of time. Reaffirm your trust in God's timing and wisdom. Let Him know you are willing to wait for His answer. Tell Him that if you need to grow in the process, you are ready. Promise to continue praying, and pray for a patient spirit as you await His reply.

PAINFULLY HONEST PRAYERS

REFLECTIONS FROM SESSION 4

1. If you have reflected on times God has graciously answered no to your prayers, tell your group about one experience God brought to mind.
2. What is one prayer for which you are still waiting for an answer? How did you feel after reaffirming your trust in God regarding this prayer request?

THE BIG PICTURE

Imagine that the mouth of a harbor at which you are standing opens up so that you can look out onto the open sea. While you are looking out on the sea, you see a huge ocean-going vessel cruising out on the shimmering waters. Just then, you hear the voice of God distinctly saying, "Climb into that fifteen-foot boat over there, cruise out of the harbor, get next to that great big ship, and tell them they are heading straight for a reef. Do whatever you have to do to get that ship to change course. If you don't do your job, they will be in trouble."

You recognize the seriousness of the situation so you climb into the little boat and make your way toward the ship. The first thing you do is position yourself in front of the ship and hold up a sign saying, "Danger, reef ahead." The ship's captain doesn't care what your little sign says and plows ahead, almost cutting your little boat in half. So then you try ramming your little boat against the side of that big ship in an effort to push it off course. Very quickly you realize that this plan, too, is futile. Finally, you find a way to board the boat and go running up to the bridge area, where you plead with the captain, saying, "I am here on a mission from God. He has told me there is a reef ahead. You had better change course or you are going to wind up endangering everyone's lives."

Thinking you are questioning his competence, the captain gets angry. You assure him, "I don't mean anything personal by this, but I'm on a mission from God. You need to turn this ship around or the results will be disastrous." Finally the captain gets so annoyed that he calls in some crew members, who push you around a little bit and lock you in the ship's meat locker. As you stand there shivering, wondering why God sent you on this mission, you hear a horrendous crash. It is the sound of steel tearing against rock. The ship begins to break apart on the reef.

A WIDE ANGLE VIEW

1

How would you feel if you were the person sent by God to stop the ship?

A BIBLICAL PORTRAIT

Read Jeremiah 20:7–18

2

In part of this prayer, Jeremiah honestly complains to God and cries out from the depths of his pain. What are some of Jeremiah's complaints to God?

Describe Jeremiah's tone and spirit in these portions of his prayer.

3 In part of this prayer, Jeremiah expresses deep trust and praise for God. What moved Jeremiah to praise?

Describe Jeremiah's tone and spirit in these portions of his prayer.

SHARPENING THE FOCUS

Read Snapshot "When the Roof Falls In"

WHEN THE ROOF FALLS IN

Jeremiah must have felt much like the man in the boat trying to stop the giant ocean liner. God called him to urge the whole nation of Israel to change its ways. If you read the book of Jeremiah, you will quickly learn that his message was not warmly received. As a matter of fact, he was rejected, beaten up, and publicly humiliated. Jeremiah was following God's leading, but the roof of his life still seemed to be caving in.

What do you do when you expect Christ's provision and protection in your life and then suddenly it seems like that protection is removed and your life has hit a reef? A routine physical turns into your worst nightmare. A marital snit goes way south and you can't seem to turn it around. Corporate restructuring costs you your job. Your child is injured in an accident. Your home is broken into. You are betrayed by a lifelong friend. What do you do when the roof falls in?

4 When Jeremiah was in this place, he prayed. Some people might read Jeremiah's prayer (20:7–18) and accuse him of being schizophrenic because he seems to be randomly jumping back and forth between deep pain and great joy. What would you say in Jeremiah's defense?

5 Describe a time in your life when the roof felt like it was caving in.

What kinds of prayers did you find yourself lifting up during this time?

Read Snapshot "Denial and Defensiveness"

DENIAL AND DEFENSIVENESS

 What do you do with the highly charged feelings that fly around in your spirit when you feel God has let you down? Some people, in an effort to be "good Christians," feel they need to protect God. They deny their pain and discount their feelings. They paste on a "Praise God anyway" smile that even a seven-year-old child could see through. They think this kind of facade makes God happy, that it's a badge of honor—a sign of spiritual maturity. They are wrong!

I remember standing with a young woman at the side of her young husband's casket. If anyone had a right to be honest about her pain before God, it was this woman. She looked at me and said, "Bill, I guess the Lord needed him in heaven more than I needed him on earth, praise God!" I think she was trying to be brave and strong, but I didn't believe a word she said. Surely the majestic God, the Creator of the universe, didn't "need" her husband in heaven or on earth. In trying to protect God, she was denying her loss and pain.

---

6 How is denial of pain and struggles a sign of being dishonest with God?

How is it an indication of being dishonest with ourselves?

7

Why are we tempted to deny our hurt, anger, and pain rather than freely admit it to God?

Read Snapshot "Painfully Honest Prayers"

PAINFULLY HONEST PRAYERS

People do a lot of different things when they feel the roof caving in on their lives. But not many people have Jeremiah's honesty. When he was in the pits, he prayed. Not a "party line" prayer, not a sanitized prayer, not a carefully edited prayer. He prayed a painfully honest prayer.

Jeremiah's heartfelt cry begins with an unedited outburst of emotion, expressing pain, anger, abandonment, and fear. Then he does a 180-degree flip and affirms the honor of being called as a prophet. He says, "I hate what is happening to me, but I love speaking the words of God and being used to impact my nation." He praises God and acknowledges His love for the needy. And then, in the next breath, Jeremiah shifts again and begins cursing the day he was born. You see, painfully honest prayers tend to be disorganized, unrehearsed, and messy. But they come from the depths of our heart and touch the heart of God.

8

What keeps you from being painfully honest in your prayers?

9

What gives you confidence to be more honest with God in prayer?

PUTTING YOURSELF IN THE PICTURE

LEARNING FROM THE PSALMS

Take time in the coming week to read Psalm 73. Seek to learn from the honesty of this prayer. Notice how it is filled with heartfelt cries of pain and struggle as well as with hope-filled declarations of praise. Seek to be free in your own prayers to lift up this kind of an honest heart.

SCRIPTURE MEMORY

Take time in the coming week to memorize these words from Psalm 62:8 about honesty in prayer:

> Trust in him at all times, O people;
> pour out your hearts to him,
> for God is our refuge.

THE LORD'S PRAYER

REFLECTIONS FROM SESSION 5

1. If you read Psalm 73 this past week, what did you learn about honesty in prayer? How has this affected the way you have prayed since our last meeting?
2. If you memorized Psalm 62:8, how has this passage impacted your trust level in God?

THE BIG PICTURE

There is an old saying, "Power corrupts and absolute power corrupts absolutely." There is something in the human heart that seems to hunger for power. Many people build their life around the pursuit of more and more power. There is nothing new in this phenomenon; it was happening even in the first century in the time of Jesus.

No one disputes the fact that Jesus Christ of Nazareth was a powerful person. He was a powerful teacher who communicated with authority. When He gave a message, there was something different about it. His words impacted lives! As a matter of fact, the book that records the words of Christ, the Bible, is still the all-time best-selling book in human history.

Jesus was also a powerful healer. He opened the eyes of the blind, made cripples walk, and brought wholeness and healing to disease ravaged people. He was a powerful provider. He stilled life-threatening storms with a word, and He even raised people from the dead. Jesus had an authority and strength that many people could not understand. The religious leaders and political power brokers of His day were threatened by how people responded to this carpenter from Nazareth.

Over a three-year period of time Jesus' followers were in close contact with Him and saw many acts of power. Somewhat predictably, their proximity to Jesus' power eventually prompted them to ask if they could redirect that power for their own agenda. In Luke 9 we find Jesus traveling from one region to another with His disciples. The most direct route would lead them through some hostile territory, so Jesus petitioned the people of this land to allow Him and His disciples free passage through the region. The people of the land flatly rejected His request. It would be like traveling from Chicago, Illinois, to Cleveland, Ohio, and being told you could not drive through Indiana. The detour would take days.

Jesus' followers became angry. They were not so concerned about the people rejecting Jesus' request as they were with the delay this would put in their travel plans. They pulled Jesus off to the side and asked Him to call on the Father's power to make fire and brimstone fall from heaven and destroy the whole region and all the people in it. Their view of prayer and the power of God was deeply confused. They were asking for capital punishment for a travel inconvenience!

A WIDE ANGLE VIEW

1 How have you seen prayer abused?

Why do so many people approach prayer with a self-seeking attitude?

A BIBLICAL PORTRAIT

Read Matthew 6:9–13

2 This prayer is a classic teaching moment in the life of Jesus. He was aware of His disciples' confusion about

prayer and wanted to set them on the right track. According to Jesus, what should we focus on when we pray?

3 Part of the reason Jesus taught this prayer was to correct some false notions the disciples had about prayer. By looking closely at the content of the Lord's Prayer, what are some of the underlying misconceptions Jesus was attacking?

How are those false views of prayer still at work?

SHARPENING THE FOCUS

Read Snapshot "Worship"

WORSHIP

The Lord's Prayer was not given for us to recite mindlessly over and over again; it was intended to provide a model of healthy, balanced prayer. Each element of this prayer turns our attention to an important dynamic of our prayer life.

The first two phrases, "Our Father in heaven" and "hallowed be your name," remind us of the centrality of worship in the life of a follower of Christ. We need to acknowledge that we are honored to be children of God. We must naturally worship Him for His greatness and thank Him for His faithfulness. "Hallowing" His name simply means giving Him rightful recognition—holding His reputation in high regard. Worship should constantly be in our hearts and on our lips.

4 What element of God's character most leads you to worship Him and pray, "Hallowed be Your name"?

5

Of all the things Jesus could have told us to begin our prayers with, why do you think He chose worship as the starting point?

Read Snapshot "Submission"

SUBMISSION

Jesus teaches us to pray, "Your will be done." God's will is already being done in heaven, but we should pray for His perfect will to be done on earth as well. More specifically, we should pray for God's will to be done in our life. This portion of Jesus' prayer centers on submission. I think Jesus was saying that before we start listing all the things we want, we need to sincerely submit ourselves to God's leading. We need to say, "I am the creature and You are the Creator. You are the potter and I am the clay." If we don't approach God with a heart of submission, it is very easy for our prayers to become self-centered and shallow."

6

If a person has a heart that is submitted to God, how will this impact the other areas mentioned in the Lord's Prayer?

Read Snapshot "Daily Bread"

DAILY BREAD

Jesus encourages us to bring our needs to the Father, knowing that He cares about us. It is important to notice that Jesus said to pray for our daily bread, not for a daily steak and lobster buffet with a forty-four-ounce soft drink and two desserts. I think His choice of bread was intentional because it is very easy to confuse our needs with our wants. God is concerned about meeting our needs. Jesus is saying, "Turn to the Father and ask for the daily provisions necessary for you to lead a God-honoring life and to support your family. Make sure you are praying for bread and not getting carried away praying for caviar." God is more than able to go beyond our needs, but it's best to leave those matters up to His discretion.

7 What are some of the "steak, lobster, and caviar" prayers we can get lured into praying?

8 What are some of the "daily bread" prayers Jesus wants us to lift to the Father?

Read Snapshot "Forgive Us"

FORGIVE US

Jesus teaches that there ought to be a component of confession in our prayers. Often the hardest two words in the human language to say are "I'm sorry." When was the last time you said, "God, before I go any further in prayer I want to list some foul-ups that happened in my life over the last twenty-four hours. I've said harsh words, had bad thoughts, been cruel in my actions, and committed many other sins. I want to confess my sins before You so I can receive grace and be restored. I don't want anything to be between us." Seeking forgiveness as well as extending forgiveness to others is critical for a healthy prayer life.

---

9 Why is regular, specific, and honest confession essential for a vital prayer life?

Read Snapshot "Protect Us"

PROTECT US

Jesus teaches us to pray, "And lead us not into temptation, but deliver us from the evil one." This component of protection should be in each one of our prayers. In the Old Testament the people lived in an agricultural society where everything revolved around farming. Sometimes farmers would plant hedges around their crops to keep the crops safe from predatory animals. Many times in the Old Testament the writers would pray, "God, put a hedge of protection around our lives." What a great image! We need to pray for God to put a hedge of protection around our lives, family, home, church, relationships, and community. The devil is trying as hard as he can to tear down our lives. We need to ask God to protect us and deliver us from his temptations.

 10 What is one area for which you need to pray for protection?

As a small group, pray for the protection of all your members.

PUTTING YOURSELF IN THE PICTURE

SCRIPTURE MEMORY

Although Jesus did not teach the Lord's Prayer so that it could be recited over and over again, it is still very meaningful to commit this prayer to memory. Having the structure of this prayer in your heart so you can expand on and personalize each aspect of it is healthy for any believer. Take time in the coming week to memorize this prayer as found in Matthew 6:9–13 from memory. Once you have learned it, use it as a springboard to a deeper prayer life:

> Our Father in heaven,
> hallowed be your name,
> your kingdom come,
> your will be done
> on earth as it is in heaven.
> Give us today our daily bread.
> Forgive us our debts,
> as we also have forgiven our debtors.
> And lead us not into temptation,
> but deliver us from the evil one.

LEADER'S NOTES

Leading a Bible discussion—especially for the first time—can make you feel both nervous and excited. If you are nervous, realize that you are in good company. Many biblical leaders, such as Moses, Joshua, and the apostle Paul, felt nervous and inadequate to lead others (see, for example, 1 Cor. 2:3). Yet God's grace was sufficient for them, just as it will be for you.

Some excitement is also natural. Your leadership is a gift to the others in the group. Keep in mind, however, that other group members also share responsibility for the group. Your role is simply to stimulate discussion by asking questions and encouraging people to respond. The suggestions listed below can help you to be an effective leader.

PREPARING TO LEAD

1. Ask God to help you understand and apply the passage to your own life. Unless that happens, you will not be prepared to lead others.
2. Carefully work through each question in the study guide. Meditate and reflect on the passage as you formulate your answers.
3. Familiarize yourself with the Leader's Notes for each session. These will help you understand the purpose of the session and will provide valuable information about the questions in the session. The Leader's Notes are not intended to be read to the group. These notes are primarily for your use as a group leader and for your preparation. However, when you find a section that relates well to your group, you may want to read a brief portion or encourage them to read this section at another time.
4. Pray for the various members of the group. Ask God to use these sessions to make you better disciples of Jesus Christ.
5. Before the first session, make sure each person has a study guide. Encourage them to prepare beforehand for each session.

LEADING THE SESSION

1. Begin the session on time. If people realize that the session begins on schedule, they will work harder to arrive on time.
2. At the beginning of your first time together, explain that these sessions are designed to be discussions, not lectures.

Encourage everyone to participate, but realize some may be hesitant to speak during the first few sessions.

3. Don't be afraid of silence. People in the group may need time to think before responding.

4. Avoid answering your own questions. If necessary, rephrase a question until it is clearly understood. Even an eager group will quickly become passive and silent if they think the leader will do most of the talking.

5. Encourage more than one answer to each question. Ask, "What do the rest of you think?" or "Anyone else?" until several people have had a chance to respond.

6. Try to be affirming whenever possible. Let people know you appreciate their insights into the passage.

7. Never reject an answer. If it is clearly wrong, ask, "Which verse led you to that conclusion?" Or let the group handle the problem by asking them what they think about the question.

8. Avoid going off on tangents. If people wander off course, gently bring them back to the passage being considered.

9. Conclude your time together with conversational prayer. Ask God to help you apply those things that you learned in the session.

10. End on time. This will be easier if you control the pace of the discussion by not spending too much time on some questions or too little on others.

We encourage all small group leaders to use *Leading Life-Changing Small Groups* (Zondervan) by Bill Donahue and the Willow Creek Small Group Team while leading their group. Developed and used by Willow Creek Community Church, this guide is an excellent resource for training and equipping followers of Christ to effectively lead small groups. It includes valuable information on how to utilize fun and creative relationship-building exercises for your group; how to plan your meeting; how to share the leadership load by identifying, developing, and working with an "apprentice leader"; and how to find creative ways to do group prayer. In addition, the book includes material and tips on handling potential conflicts and difficult personalities, forming group covenants, inviting new members, improving listening skills, studying the Bible, and much more. Using *Leading Life-Changing Small Groups* will help you create a group that members love to be a part of.

Now let's discuss the different elements of this small group study guide and how to use them for the session portion of your group meeting.

ᴛᴇ Big Picture

ᴌach session will begin with a short story or overview of the
lesson theme. This is called "The Big Picture" because it intro-
duces the central theme of the session. You will need to read
this section as a group or have group members read it on their
own before discussion begins. Here are three ways you can
approach this section of the small group session:

- As the group leader, read this section out loud for the
  whole group and then move into the questions in the next
  section, "A Wide Angle View." (You might read the first
  week, but then use the other two options below to encourage group involvement.)
- Ask a group member to volunteer to read this section for
  the group. This allows another group member to participate. It is best to ask someone in advance to give them time
  to read over the section before reading it to the group. It is
  also good to ask someone to volunteer, and not to assign
  this task. Some people do not feel comfortable reading in
  front of a group. After a group member has read this section out loud, move into the discussion questions.
- Allow time at the beginning of the session for each person
  to read this section silently. If you do this, be sure to allow
  enough time for everyone to finish reading so they can
  think about what they've read and be ready for meaningful
  discussion.

A Wide Angle View

This section includes one or more questions that move the
group into a general discussion of the session topic. These
questions are designed to help group members begin dis-
cussing the topic in an open and honest manner. Once the
topic of the lesson has been established, move on to the Bible
passage for the session.

A Biblical Portrait

This portion of the session includes a Scripture reading and
one or more questions that help group members see how the
theme of the session is rooted and based in biblical teaching.
The Scripture reading can be handled just like "The Big Picture" section: You can read it for the group, have a group
member read it, or allow time for silent reading. Make sure
everyone has a Bible or that you have Bibles available for

those who need them. Once you have read the passage, ask the question(s) in this section so that group members can dig into the truth of the Bible.

SHARPENING THE FOCUS

The majority of the discussion questions for the session are in this section. These questions are practical and help group members apply biblical teaching to their daily lives.

SNAPSHOTS

The "Snapshots" in each session help prepare group members for discussion. These anecdotes give additional insight to the topic being discussed. Each "Snapshot" should be read at a designated point in the session. This is clearly marked in the session as well as in the Leader's Notes. Again, follow the same format as you do with "The Big Picture" section and the "Biblical Portrait" section: Either you read the anecdote, have a group member volunteer to read, or provide time for silent reading. However you approach this section, you will find these anecdotes very helpful in triggering lively dialogue and moving discussion in a meaningful direction.

PUTTING YOURSELF IN THE PICTURE

Here's where you roll up your sleeves and put the truth into action. This portion is very practical and action-oriented. At the end of each session there will be suggestions for one or two ways group members can put what they've just learned into practice. Review the action goals at the end of each session and challenge group members to work on one or more of them in the coming week.

You will find follow-up questions for the "Putting Yourself in the Picture" section at the beginning of the next week's session. Starting with the second week, there will be time set aside at the beginning of the session to look back and talk about how you have tried to apply God's Word in your life since your last time together.

PRAYER

You will want to open and close your small group with a time of prayer. Occasionally, there will be specific direction within a session for how you can do this. Most of the time, however, you will need to decide the best place to stop and pray. You

y want to pray or have a group member volunteer to begin
e lesson with a prayer. Or you might want to read "The Big
Picture" and discuss the "Wide Angle View" questions before
opening in prayer. In some cases, it might be best to open in
prayer after you have read the Bible passage. You need to
decide where you feel an opening prayer best fits for your
group.

When opening in prayer, think in terms of the session theme
and pray for group members (including yourself) to be
responsive to the truth of Scripture and the working of the
Holy Spirit. If you have seekers in your group (people investi-
gating Christianity but not yet believers) be sensitive to your
expectations for group prayer. Seekers may not yet be ready
to take part in group prayer.

Be sure to close your group with a time of prayer as well. One
option is for you to pray for the entire group. Or you might
allow time for group members to offer audible prayers that
others can agree with in their hearts. Another approach
would be to allow a time of silence for one-on-one prayers
with God and then to close this time with a simple "Amen."

THE PRIVILEGE OF PRAYER

LUKE 18:1—8

INTRODUCTION

It has been my experience that if people listen carefully to the story Jesus told in Luke 18, they will be motivated to pray. Those who have not been praying enough start praying. Frustrated prayers unclench their fists, open their hands toward heaven, and cry out to God. Brazen, nonprayers find themselves terribly tempted to give prayer a try. Embarrassed beginners lose their embarrassment and just plunge in. And veteran prayers gladly sign up for another tour of duty. When we realize that God has given us direct access to His throne room and that He loves to hear our prayers, we want to dial in on a regular basis and grow in our prayer lives.

THE BIG PICTURE

Take time to read this introduction with the group. There are suggestions for how this can be done in the beginning of the leader's section.

A WIDE ANGLE VIEW

Question One Every member in your group will have different responses to the topic of prayer. They will also have different mental images of prayer that are connected to their past. There are no right or wrong answers to these questions. Some will have negative memories and feelings; others will have positive feelings. The key is to allow the various feelings to surface as you begin this session on prayer.

A BIBLICAL PORTRAIT

Read Luke 18:1–8

Read Snapshot "A Contrast, *Not* a Comparison" before Question 2

Questions Two & Three Over the years, people have read the story of the widow and the judge in a sincere attempt to

...arn something that will motivate them to pray. After doing a little thinking about the story, some conclude that the story is an allegory, or a comparison. In other words, we humans are like the widow in the story—weak, powerless, without status, abandoned, and hopeless. Because of our condition, we have to seek help from above.

Continuing with this allegory, we could go on to say that God is like the judge in the story. He has planets to spin, harps to keep in tune, and lots of things to do that are more important than worrying about our petty little needs. If we do dare to bother Him with our prayers, it is like banging on the doors of heaven until God gets sick of the noise: If we keep it up long enough, sooner or later we will manage to wrench a blessing from the closed hands of a God who doesn't want to give it. Sooner or later God will shout, "I can't take it anymore. Gabriel, Michael, fix this guy. Fix this woman."

In the snapshot we saw the other side to reading this story—as a contrast. In looking at the story this way, we learn that we are nothing like the widow and that God is nothing like the judge. We discover that God wants to answer our prayers and bless us. We have an open invitation to God's presence because He has given us a direct line. We are His favored children.

SHARPENING THE FOCUS

Read Snapshot "A Direct Line" before Question 4

Question Four Listen to the following phrase: *No one's voice sounds sweeter to God than your voice.* If you really let the impact of this phrase sink in, you can bet it will motivate you to pray. Too often we focus on our mistakes and foul-ups. Our commitment sags, our convictions are out of line, and we feel distant. We forget how much we matter to God, and we start to feel He really does not want to hear from us. It is in the middle of these very times that we need to remember we are in a favored position in the family of God. We have direct, private access to the Father. No one's voice is sweeter to God's ears than ours.

Read Snapshot "The Heart of God" before Question 5

Question Five God is interested in our prayers because He is supremely interested in us. God has this universe functioning just fine. To Him the most important thing in the cosmos is what is going on in your life. You and me, his favored children, are what preoccupies the attention of God. We don't have to pester Him to get His attention. We don't have to grovel or groan or bug God into answering our prayers.

If one of my kids ever called me and said, "Dad, please, please, please, I beg of you, I petition you, please listen to my need or my concern," I would say, "Time out. You don't have to go through all of that. Remember who you are and who I am. As my family, you are the most important people in my life. Just talk to me." I would say to my daughter or my son, "You are my child. You already have my heart and my ear. I care about the big things and the little things, because when it comes to you, there are no little things."

God, too, is saying, "You already have My heart and My ear. I am supremely interested in you, so pray with confidence. Pray about big stuff, pray about little stuff. Pray in the morning, in the afternoon, in the evening. I will hear you wherever you pray."

Question Six God is sovereignly able to respond to the concerns we bring to Him. Suffice it to say, if creation wasn't a problem, if stilling a storm wasn't a problem, and if resurrecting Jesus was not a problem, your problem is not too big for God to handle.

Telling stories of God's provision is a great reminder to group members that God is still in the business of hearing and answering prayers.

Question Eight God cares about our needs and concerns, no matter how big or small. He can handle them. Take time as a group to communicate some of the things you are praying about at this time in your life. Be sure to encourage group members to write down these needs and pray for them in the week ahead.

PUTTING YOURSELF IN THE PICTURE

Tell group members you will be providing time at the beginning of the next meeting for them to discuss how they have put their faith into action. Let them tell their stories. However, don't limit their interaction to the two options provided. They may have put themselves into the picture in some other way as a result of your study. Allow for honest and open communication.

Also, be clear that there will not be any kind of a "test" or forced reporting. All you are going to do is allow time for people to volunteer to talk about how they have applied what

ey learned in your last study. Some group members will feel
pressured if they think you are going to make everyone provide a "report." You don't want anyone to skip the next group
because they are afraid of having to say they did not follow
up on what they learned from the prior session. Focus instead
on providing a place for honest communication without cre-
ating pressure and fear of being embarrassed.

Every session from this point on will open with a look back at
the "Putting Yourself in the Picture" section of the previous
session.

HOW TO PRAY AUTHENTICALLY

MATTHEW 6:5–8

INTRODUCTION

I don't know of another passage in Scripture that speaks as straightforwardly to the issue of how to pray than Matthew 6:5–13. The advice Jesus offers to His followers concerning how to pray could be ordered in three clear statements: pray secretly, sincerely, and specifically. These three guidelines will give us a strong start as we seek to become people of authentic prayer.

THE BIG PICTURE

Take time to read this introduction with the group. There are suggestions for how this can be done in the beginning of the leader's section.

A BIBLICAL PORTRAIT

Read Matthew 6:5–8

Question Two Christ warns that God is not interested in inauthentic prayer. We are to avoid public displays of prayer that are intended to impress others and gain their approval. Prayer should be directed to God, not to other people. He also calls His followers to avoid insincere repetition of mindless prayers. He does not want us thinking that heaping up a bunch of religious phrases equals prayer. Vague and general religious platitudes are not what touch the heart of God.

Question Three Jesus tells us that authentic prayer comes out of a quiet place where we will not be distracted and where we can meet God without worrying about what everyone else is thinking about us. Authentic prayer is also dynamic. It is not the stagnant repetition of worn-out religious phrases; it is the cry of a heart that sincerely wants to talk with its Creator. Authentic prayer is also specific (see vv. 9–13). Jesus calls us to pray with an eye to detail. We should lift up specific praise, needs, confession, and thanks.

ЅHARPENING THE FOCUS

Read Snapshot "Pray Secretly" before Question 4

Question Four I know some married couples who have favorite restaurants where they go and have special nights out. They love the atmosphere. They have a favorite table. They look forward to going there and they return often. It is a special place where they can really talk with each other.

Likewise, I know some families who have special vacation spots that are almost like second homes. Great things happen when their families are in these places. These are places filled with special memories.

A special place where you meet with God can have this same dynamic. For me, this place is in my office near the left corner of my credenza. I have an open Bible there and a crown of thorns a friend gave me to remind me of the suffering of my Savior. I also have a shepherd's staff that I sometimes hold up during the supplication section of my prayer time. And I also have a little sign that says, "God is able."

This place has become holy for me; it's my inner room. I go there early in the morning when there are no distractions. It is where I pour my heart to God, where I worship him. It is where I pray for the members of the church God has called me to pastor. This place is extremely significant to me. There is no other place that feels so much like home when it comes to praying.

Jesus wants us to find a quiet place—a secret place—where we will not be distracted. Do you have such a place? It can be a basement utility room, a pantry in the kitchen, a barn, an office, the front seat of a car or pickup truck. Try out more than one if you like. Once you have your "quiet place," you can learn how to commune with your Lord on a regular basis.

Read Snapshot "Pray Sincerely" before Question 6

Question Six Jesus calls us to pray sincerely. He says, "Don't just get caught up in phrases, in pious-sounding sentences, clichés, and meaningless repetition."

We must be on the lookout for autopilot prayers. This was brought home to me dramatically some years ago when I attended a conference in Colorado to which several Christian leaders were invited. The level of conversation was so high that I was straining to keep up with all the theology and philosophy being tossed around.

One of the evenings we gathered in a little restaurant called "The Hole in the Wall" for dinner. When the food was served, one of the seminary professors asked another participant to pray. We all bowed our heads and I braced myself for a lofty prayer that belonged in a theology class. Instead, the guy began, "Father, I love being alive today, and I love sitting down with brothers in this restaurant eating good food and talking about kingdom business. I know You are at this table, and I am glad. I want to tell You in front of these brothers that I love You and I will do anything You ask me to do." He went on just talking like this to God, and when he said "Amen," I thought, *I have some growing to do.* Too often we pray autopilot prayers when God wants us to lift up prayers that are sincere.

Question Seven This can be a touchy subject, because many churches pray this prayer every week in worship. Some people pray it every day at a meal or in their own prayer time. However, be honest about how you feel God intends this prayer to be used. In light of the context of Jesus' teaching (Matt. 6:7–8), how should we use this prayer?

Read Snapshot "Pray Specifically" before Question 8

Questions Eight, Nine, & Ten You may want to use the prayers communicated in response to these questions to form a prayer list for the coming week. You may also want to point out, after group members have responded to these questions, that they have been praying. You see, some group members might not be willing to say anything if you ask them to pray for each of these areas. However, when you ask them to communicate their response to these three questions, they are actually praying . . . God hears every word they say! After a time of open sharing, let your group know you have just had a prayer time lifting up adoration, thanksgiving, and supplication!

PUTTING YOURSELF IN THE PICTURE

Challenge group members to take time in the coming week to use part or all of this application section as an opportunity for continued growth.

DANGEROUS PRAYERS

PSALM 139:1—12, 23—24

INTRODUCTION

This lessons moves us to the graduate school level of prayer. Often we offer up prayers that focus on our needs. This kind of prayer is important, but when we focus on only what we need or want, our prayer lives become very one-dimensional. When we enter the realm of dangerous prayers, we are asking God to work a transformation within us. Our focus is not on what we gain, but on His presence in our lives. In this session we will focus on four dangerous prayers: "search me," "break me," "stretch me," and "lead me."

THE BIG PICTURE

Take time to read this introduction with the group. There are suggestions for how this can be done in the beginning of the leader's section.

A WIDE ANGLE VIEW

Question One All of us have some experience with this thing called prayer. Some people learned to pray as they watched parents, grandparents, or church members lift up deeply sincere prayers. Others struggled to learn to pray on their own. Invite group members to recount their experiences of learning to pray. Some might remember such stories with fondness and nostalgia; others might have painful memories. The key is to be honest in telling your own stories.

A BIBLICAL PORTRAIT

Read Psalm 139:1–12, 23–24

Read Snapshot "Search Me" before Question 2

Question Two In this Psalm David extols God for being present everywhere. He says, "Wherever I walk on this planet I will never be alone, because You are present wherever I go." As

David recognizes that God knows everything and made every thing, he also declares His greatness. He says, "You are a powerful God. You made everything, and I will give thanks to You."

Then a thought strikes David. He realizes that God thinks about David's personal life all day long. He says, "How precious are Your thoughts about me, oh God. If I were to count Your thoughts about me, they would outnumber the grains of sand of the seashores." David is caught up in the wonder of it all.

David realizes that God can see him through and through. There is no hiding from God. But he still takes a risk in asking God to shine the burning light of His holiness on the darkest corners of his heart. David wants nothing hidden from God. He is entering the level of dangerous prayer.

Sometimes when I am praying, I am forced to do the same thing David did. I realize there are pockets of resistance and rebellion within me and I have to decide if I am going to pray a dangerous prayer. Finally I say, "Search me, oh God. Turn the spotlight on me. Know my heart. Expose any waywardness inside of me."

When was the last time you really prayed a "search me" prayer? It is like the saying in business: "Don't ask the question if you don't want to hear the answer." Don't pray this kind of prayer unless you are humble enough before God to receive the answer. Because God, by His Holy Spirit, will turn the searchlight on. Something will get exposed, and then you will need to deal with it.

SHARPENING THE FOCUS

Read Snapshot "Break Me" before Question 4

Question Four In the eighth chapter of the gospel of John a woman is caught in the act of adultery and is dragged in front of Jesus. The religious leaders hope Jesus will condemn her, but instead Jesus turns the tide of their judgment and condemns the religious leaders for their hypocrisy. Jesus extends forgiveness to the woman and calls her to repent of her sin. Do you remember the last words Jesus said to the woman? Let me paraphrase it: "Go your way, but you better break this pattern because it dishonors God and will destroy your life."

Another time Jesus had dinner with an extortioner—a man whose goal in life was to accumulate money, even if it meant stealing from the poor. He was a tax collector named Zacchaeus. After Zacchaeus's dramatic and life-changing encounter with Jesus, he became a changed man. He was committed to

...eaking the pattern of financial dishonesty that had been rul-
...ng his life. He announced publicly, "I am going to pay back
everyone I have cheated, and I will also give away much of
my money to the poor." God is still in the business of breaking
us so He can use us.

Read Snapshot "Stretch Me" before Question 5

Question Five It rarely feels good to be stretched. As a matter
of fact, it almost always hurts. In the process of being stretched,
we often wonder if it is worth the pain. Still, stretching is part
of the process of spiritual growth. Maturity does not come
easy. When a time of stretching is over, we can often look back
and thank God for bringing us through such a growth process.
It takes real courage to actually invite a time of spiritual stretching, but it is always a life-changing experience.

Read Snapshot "Lead Me" before Question 7

Questions Seven & Eight Hearing others tell of how God
has led their lives is an inspirational experience. It reminds us
that God is still in the business of directing the lives of His
people. Celebrate the stories of God's faithful leading in the
lives of your group members.

Prayer Note: You should encourage your group members to
write down the prayer areas communicated during this session. You will notice that there is an invitation to express
some risky and dangerous prayer needs in questions four, six,
and eight. As you close your small group, it might be very
appropriate to spend some time praying for each other. Use
these three areas of prayer needs to guide your time.

Putting Yourself in the Picture

Challenge group members to take time in the coming week to
use part or all of this application section as an opportunity for
continued growth.

THE MYSTERY OF UNANSWERED PRAYER

MARK 10:35–45

INTRODUCTION

I have to credit a pastor friend of mine for his insight on this subject and for my outline of this session. If you've been praying and nothing seems to be happening, think about these statements with reference to unanswered prayer. If the request is wrong, God will say no to your request. If the timing is wrong, God might choose to say, "Go slow"—slow down and wait on His leading. But if the request is right, the timing is right, and you are right, chances are God will say, "Let's go." It is often hard to discern exactly what is happening when our prayers seem unanswered, but this little outline will help us begin to understand more about this important topic.

THE BIG PICTURE

Take time to read this introduction with the group. There are suggestions for how this can be done in the beginning of the leader's section.

A WIDE ANGLE VIEW

Question One We have all prayed prayers that we later wished we had not prayed. Certainly, the disciples felt like this on a number of occasions. They would ask Jesus to do something and, before you knew it, they were wishing they had never opened their mouths. Sometimes, in retrospect, we actually thank God for answering no to our prayers.

A BIBLICAL PORTRAIT

Read Mark 10:35–45

Questions Two & Three James and John had a way of opening their mouths and inserting their feet. In this passage

...y made a huge request of Jesus that was met with an ...mphatic, "No!" As a matter of fact, Jesus followed up their selfish request with a powerful lesson on humility and serving others. After Jesus finished teaching, the disciples must have had deep insight as to why He said no to their request. In the same way, we too can learn a great deal from the times God says no to our requests.

SHARPENING THE FOCUS

Read Snapshot "If the Request Is Wrong, God Says, 'No!'" before Question 4

Questions Four & Five I remember a time when the elders of our church had been dealing with a particular need on our staff. We knew we needed just the right person and we all thought of the same individual at the same time. We agreed that we were going to really pray and trust that this was the right person for our staff.

I was commissioned to meet him and offer him the position. The two of us met for lunch and I prayed for God to lead me. As I was just ready to extend the invitation, it became apparent to me that God was saying, "Don't do it." By God's grace, I decided not to offer the person the job. I went back and told the elders I couldn't do it. Six months later we learned that there was deception in the life of that leader. His entire ministry crumbled around him. God, in His wisdom, answered our prayer with a clear, "No."

If you have been praying diligently about a matter, and if you have sensed resistance from heaven, take time to review your request. Maybe it is destructive in ways you don't understand. Maybe it is self-serving or shortsighted. It might even be too small. Or God could have something better in mind. If the request is wrong, God will say no.

Read Snapshot "If the Timing Is Wrong, God Says, 'Slow!'" before Question 6

Question Six God's delays are not necessarily God's denials. Sometimes God says, "Not quite yet. Trust Me. I know what I am doing. I have My reasons. Slow down and wait for Me." We need to remember that we are the creatures, God is the Creator. His ways are higher than our ways, and His thoughts are higher than our thoughts. We need to wait for His timing.

Be wary in insisting that you know better than God does when a prayer request should be granted. God has His reasons for saying, "Not yet." He may want you to develop more endurance, trust, patience, or submission. He may well have concerns beyond your needs—how this activity will impact others. As human beings, we tend to be much more concerned about comfort and convenience than about building character through patiently waiting on God's timing. Sometimes the prayers that are sweetest to have answered are the ones you have lifted to God for a long, long time.

Read Snapshot "If You Are Wrong, God Will Say, 'Grow!'" before Question 7

Question Seven One time in the Old Testament, despite clear instruction from God to offer only the best lambs for sacrifices, the Israelites decided to give the worst lambs in their flocks. They gave God the lame and the blind lambs, and then sold the good ones for top dollar in the marketplace. God spoke through the prophet Malachi and asked the Israelites why they were disobeying Him and still asking for His favor and blessing. It made no sense then, and it makes no sense now. Galatians 6:7 says, "Do not be deceived: God cannot be mocked. A man reaps what he sows."

Sometimes the only obstacle standing in the way of our receiving a desperately needed answer from God is us. The request may not be wrong. The timing might be fine. But when *we* are wrong, God says, "The biggest concern on My heart right now is your growth. Deal with your sin. It is the only thing standing in the way. Change your attitude. Stop that practice. End that pattern. Reconcile that relationship. Repent, receive forgiveness, and grow."

Question Eight Take time for silent reflection to listen for the still, small voice of the Spirit. Encourage group members to invite God's inspection in their life and heart. Gently open the door for group members to communicate what God has put on their heart. If someone risks sharing on this level, pray for that person and extend support and care.

PUTTING YOURSELF IN THE PICTURE

Challenge group members to take time in the coming week to use part or all of this application section as an opportunity for continued growth.

PAINFULLY HONEST PRAYERS

JEREMIAH 20:7—18

INTRODUCTION

Sometimes our prayers are so tidy and sanitized that God must wonder if our heart is connected to our mouth. He knows our pain, sorrow, anger, hurt, and struggles, yet when we pray, too often we push these feelings down and try to present only the positive. We may feel that expressing our anger or hurt might be offensive to God. Or maybe we were raised to bury those feelings and never let anyone see them.

Well, guess what? God knows us and He still loves us. We matter to Him and He wants to hear about everything that is on our heart. It is time we learn to lift up painfully honest prayers, understanding that they are not painful to God. What makes them painful is how hard it can be for us to tell the truth, even to our God.

THE BIG PICTURE

Take time to read this introduction with the group. There are suggestions for how this can be done in the beginning of the leader's section.

A BIBLICAL PORTRAIT

Read Jeremiah 20:7–18

Question Two Jeremiah began fulfilling God's assignment by talking to the rulers, priests, and merchants. He said, "You know, I got a message for you from God. God sees your corruption, your wickedness, your self-centeredness. He sees how you are rebelling against Him. He wants you to turn things around and repent. He wants you to receive forgiveness and go a new direction as a nation and as individuals."

To make a long story short, the rulers, priests, and merchants laughed Jeremiah right out of town. They said, in effect, "You are not from God. We don't have a problem. Beat it."

This discouraged Jeremiah, but he decided to approach them again. This time he went into graphic detail, saying, "In the past, when God warned His people and they repented, they received forgiveness and experienced the blessings of God. But when they ignored the prophets, judgment came upon them. I plead with you, repent and change course."

For the second time the rulers, priests, and merchants said, "We are telling you, get lost! We don't think you are from God, we don't have a problem." And then, to top it off, they not only rejected Jeremiah, they beat him up and publicly humiliated him.

At this point Jeremiah's feelings were churning. So he poured them all out to God. All his anger, fear, sadness, confusion, regret, depression, and feelings of betrayal. He did not hold anything back.

Question Three Jeremiah also lifted up deep personal prayers of praise. In the middle of his pain he still knew the goodness of God. At one moment his tone was depressed and sad, and the next moment he was confident and rejoicing in his God. The depth of Jeremiah's honesty in prayer led him to transparent expression of his sorrow and joy, his anger and praise. We can learn a great deal from Jeremiah's example.

Sharpening the Focus

Read Snapshot "When the Roof Falls In" before Question 4

Questions Four & Five When we don't feel free to be honest with God, our prayers are often neatly organized presentations of our praises and needs packaged in safe words and phrases. When we realize that God wants us to pour our heart out to Him, our prayers are not nearly as neat and tidy.

Jeremiah was not schizophrenic, he was just honest. Even though his prayers poured out of a broken heart, he still trusted in God. His cries were honest expressions of the depth of his despair that was still rooted in his confidence in God's power and faithfulness. When we become honest with God, we will discover that our prayers, too, will span the heights of praise and worship as well as the depths of sorrow and pain.

Read Snapshot "Denial and Defensiveness" before Question 6

Questions Six & Seven When some people feel God has treated them unfairly, they deny their true feelings, discount

eir pain, and try to protect God. With a plastic smile on their
ace they try to press on and "be strong." Other people who
are stung by what seems to be a breakdown in God's protection simply pull back from ever really trusting God again.
They start to relate to God in a guarded, detached kind of
way. They become numb both spiritually and relationally, no
longer fully engaging in life, faith, or relationships. Still others
spin on their heels, thumb their nose at God, and say, "I was a
fool to believe all of this. I should have known we are on our
own down here. You don't protect us from anything." Sadly,
many people who once trusted God have defected and gone
AWOL because they never learned to be honest in their
prayers.

Read Snapshot "Painfully Honest Prayers" before Question 8

Questions Eight & Nine When I first read this prayer, I jok-
ingly thought to myself, "Don't hold back, Jeremiah. Tell God
how you really feel!" But the joke was on me. After studying
this passage closely, I realized Jeremiah felt free to pour his
heart out because he was so sure of God's character and love.
Jeremiah was so convinced that God's presence was a safe
place that he could risk praying a painfully honest prayer. He
believed God could handle a messy prayer. He knew God was
interested in all his feelings, even the tough ones. Jeremiah
believed God was a refuge, even for those with chaos in their
hearts.

Are you that convinced of the character of God? Can you risk
praying a painfully honest prayer? Do you really view God's
presence as a safe place? When you do, you will learn to pray
with real honesty.

If you want to take a risk and learn to pray with honesty, start
by getting away to a quiet place with God. Don't rehearse
your prayer. Simply say, "Hang on, God, because I am going
to say some things I should have said to you a long time ago."
And then let it rip! Tell God everything that is on your heart.
Don't sanitize it, organize it, or edit it. Tell him everything.

After you have finished, pause and say, "Now God, You
heard all of my stuff. What do You want to teach me?" Ask
Him some specific questions: "What new perspective do You
have for me?" "How can I change in my life to live more for
You?" "What can I accept to help me follow Your will?"
"What challenge should I embark upon?" "What can I learn
through what I am experiencing?" Then commit yourself to

remaining honest with God as part of your lifestyle. Let th. become a natural part of your prayer life.

PUTTING YOURSELF IN THE PICTURE

Challenge group members to take time in the coming week to use part or all of this application section as an opportunity for continued growth.

THE LORD'S PRAYER

MATTHEW 6:9–13

INTRODUCTION

There is power in prayer. Anyone who has prayed for a long period of time will tell you how God has miraculously unleashed His power through prayer. Terry Anderson, a U.S. citizen who was held hostage for over six years was asked, "How did you stand up to all the horror associated with being a hostage?" Do you know what he said? "I am a Christian. I prayed. The power of God sustained me." In both the little and the big things in life, prayer has the power to make a dramatic difference.

THE BIG PICTURE

Take time to read this introduction with the group. There are suggestions for how this can be done in the beginning of the leader's section.

A WIDE ANGLE VIEW

Question One Having access to divine power can be dangerous because it can lead to deceitful prayers and manipulative prayers.

There are many examples of prayer abuse. Stan is a chronic overspender. His credit cards are all tapped to the limit. He has never had a budget. He likes looking at the centerfolds of Sharper Image catalogs and drools over everything that shines. Now the creditors are knocking at his doors and he is in real trouble. So Stan, who is a Christian, finally retreats to his bedroom, falls to his knees, and asks God to bail him out. "I need a higher paying job," he pleads. "I need insight on lottery numbers. I need a dramatic answer to this prayer in the form of cash, and I need it now!" That is prayer abuse. A better prayer for Stan is, "Dear God, help me face the truth about myself. Something is broken inside of me that I am trying to fix by buying stuff that shines and sparkles. I am dishonoring You, and my life is out of control. Help me discern why I don't have the basic tools for self-control and budgeting. Help me understand why I can't live within my means. God, give me the courage to take the steps I need to face this problem and to have victory over it." That is a God-honoring prayer!

A Biblical Portrait

Read Matthew 6:9–13

Questions Two through Ten The rest of this lesson focuses on the Lord's Prayer. At the close of your group you may want to spend a time of prayer together. Depending on your group, you may want to invite people to pray out loud at appropriate times or you can walk them through this prayer and have them lift up their hearts silently to God. I would challenge you as a leader to encourage group members to pray out loud together so they can support each other in prayer.

Use the structure of the Lord's Prayer as directed below to guide your group through a time of prayer:

Heavenly Father, Your son taught us to pray:

Our Father in heaven,
hallowed be your name,

Hear us now as we lift our prayers of praise and worship to You.

(Leave time for group members to pray prayers of worship.)

You also call us to seek Your will in our lives. You want us to pray:

your kingdom come,
your will be done
on earth as it is in heaven.

Hear us as we pray for Your will in our lives, our homes, our careers, our community, and in Your church.

(Leave time for group members to pray for God's will in their lives.)

Jesus taught us to pray:

Give us today our daily bread.

Hear us as we pray for Your provision of our needs.

(Leave time for group members to lift needs in prayer.)

We have sinned against You, God, and You taught us to pray:

orgive us our debts,
as we also have forgiven our debtors.

Hear us as we silently confess our sins to You.

(Leave a time of silence for personal confession.)

You are powerful, and You are able to protect us, and You have told us to pray:

And lead us not into temptation,
but deliver us from the evil one.

Hear us as we pray for your protection over our lives.

(Leave time for prayers of protection.)

Thank you, Heavenly Father, for how You love Your children. We lift this prayer in the name of Jesus Christ, Your Son and our Lord.

PUTTING YOURSELF IN THE PICTURE

Challenge group members to take time in the coming week to use part or all of this application section as an opportunity for continued growth.

ADDITIONAL WILLOW CREEK RESOURCES

Small Group Resources

Coaching Life-Changing Small Group Leaders, by Bill Donahue and Greg Bowman
The Complete Book of Questions, by Garry Poole
The Connecting Church, by Randy Frazee
Leading Life-Changing Small Groups, by Bill Donahue and the Willow Creek Team
The Seven Deadly Sins of Small Group Ministry, by Bill Donahue and Russ Robinson
Walking the Small Group Tightrope, by Bill Donahue and Russ Robinson

Evangelism Resources

Becoming a Contagious Christian (book), by Bill Hybels and Mark Mittelberg
The Case for a Creator, by Lee Strobel
The Case for Christ, by Lee Strobel
The Case for Faith, by Lee Strobel
Seeker Small Groups, by Garry Poole
The Three Habits of Highly Contagious Christians, by Garry Poole

Spiritual Gifts and Ministry

Network Revised (training course), by Bruce Bugbee and Don Cousins
The Volunteer Revolution, by Bill Hybels
What You Do Best in the Body of Christ—Revised, by Bruce Bugbee

Marriage and Parenting

Fit to Be Tied, by Bill and Lynne Hybels
Surviving a Spiritual Mismatch in Marriage, by Lee and Leslie Strobel

Ministry Resources

An Hour on Sunday, by Nancy Beach
Building a Church of Small Groups, by Bill Donahue and Russ Robinson
The Heart of the Artist, by Rory Noland
Making Your Children's Ministry the Best Hour of Every Kid's Week, by Sue Miller and David Staal
Thriving as an Artist in the Church, by Rory Noland

Curriculum

An Ordinary Day with Jesus, by John Ortberg and Ruth Haley Barton
Becoming a Contagious Christian (kit), by Mark Mittelberg, Lee Strobel, and Bill Hybels
Good Sense Budget Course, by Dick Towner, John Tofilon, and the Willow Creek Team
If You Want to Walk on Water, You've Got to Get Out of the Boat, by John Ortberg with Stephen and Amanda Sorenson
The Life You've Always Wanted, by John Ortberg with Stephen and Amanda Sorenson
The Old Testament Challenge, by John Ortberg with Kevin and Sherry Harney, Mindy Caliguire, and Judson Poling

WILLOW
Willow Creek Association

Willow Creek Association
Vision, Training, Resources for Prevailing Churches

This resource was created to serve you and to help you build a local church that prevails. It is just one of many ministry tools that are part of the Willow Creek Resources® line, published by the Willow Creek Association together with Zondervan.

The Willow Creek Association (WCA) was created in 1992 to serve a rapidly growing number of churches from across the denominational spectrum that are committed to helping unchurched people become fully devoted followers of Christ. Membership in the WCA now numbers over 12,000 Member Churches worldwide from more than ninety denominations.

The Willow Creek Association links like-minded Christian leaders with each other and with strategic vision, training, and resources in order to help them build prevailing churches designed to reach their redemptive potential. Here are some of the ways the WCA does that.

- **The Leadership Summit**—a once a year, two-and-a-half-day conference to envision and equip Christians with leadership gifts and responsibilities. Presented live at Willow Creek as well as via satellite broadcast to over 130 locations across North America, this event is designed to increase the leadership effectiveness of pastors, ministry staff, volunteer church leaders, and Christians in the marketplace.

- **Ministry-Specific Conferences**—throughout each year the WCA hosts a variety of conferences and training events—both at Willow Creek's main campus and offsite, across the U.S., and around the world—targeting church leaders and volunteers in ministry-specific areas such as: small groups, preaching and teaching, the arts, children, students, volunteers, stewardship, etc.

- **Willow Creek Resources®**—provides churches with trusted and field-tested ministry resources in such areas as leadership, evangelism, spiritual formation, spiritual gifts, small groups, stewardship, student ministry, children's ministry, the use of the arts—drama, media, contemporary music—and more.

- **WCA Member Benefits**—includes substantial discounts to WCA training events, a 20 percent discount on all Willow Creek Resources®, *Defining Moments* monthly audio journal for leaders, quarterly *Willow* magazine, access to a Members-Only section on WillowNet, monthly communications, and more. Member Churches also receive special discounts and premier services through WCA's growing number of ministry partners—Select Service Providers—and save an average of $500 annually depending on the level of engagement.

For specific information about WCA conferences, resources, membership, and other ministry services contact:

Willow Creek Association
P.O. Box 3188
Barrington, IL 60011-3188
Phone: 847-570-9812
Fax: 847-765-5046
www.willowcreek.com

Continue building your new community!
New Community Series

Bill Hybels and John Ortberg
with Kevin and Sherry Harney

Exodus: Journey Toward God 978-0-310-22771-7

Parables: Imagine Life God's Way 978-0-310-22881-3

Sermon on the Mount1: Connect with God 978-0-310-22884-4

Sermon on the Mount2: Connect with Others 978-0-310-22883-7

Acts: Build Community 978-0-310-22770-0

Romans: Find Freedom 978-0-310-22765-6

Philippians: Run the Race 978-0-310-23314-5

Colossians: Discover the New You 978-0-310-22769-4

James: Live Wisely 978-0-310-22767-0

1 Peter: Stand Strong 978-0-310-22773-1

1 John: Love Each Other 978-0-310-22768-7

Revelation: Experience God's Power 978-0-310-22882-0

Look for New Community at your local Christian bookstore.

Continue the Transformation
Pursuing Spiritual Transformation

John Ortberg, Laurie Pederson,
and Judson Poling

Grace: An Invitation to a Way of Life 978-0-310-22074-9

Growth: Training vs. Trying 978-0-310-22075-6

Groups: The Life-Giving Power of Community 978-0-310-22076-3

Gifts: The Joy of Serving God 978-0-310-22077-0

Giving: Unlocking the Heart of Good Stewardship 978-0-310-22078-7

Fully Devoted: Living Each Day in Jesus' Name 978-0-310-22073-2

Look for Pursuing Spiritual Transformation at your local Christian bookstore.

Tough Questions
Garry Poole and Judson Poling

Softcover

Reality Check Series
by Mark Ashton

We want to hear from you. Please send your comments about this book to us in care of zreview@zondervan.com. Thank you.

ZONDERVAN.com/
AUTHORTRACKER
follow your favorite authors